How To Get YOUR Solicitor's Training Contract

How to prepare for and ace the application form and interview for a solicitor's training contract

By James Howard

Copyright

Copyright

Chapter 1

Introduction

Congratulations! By buying this book you are already one big step ahead of many others considering a career in law. If you want to give yourself the best chance of getting a training contract, this is a must read.

In today's volatile economic climate the demand for positions in law firms has never been higher, with graduates that once would have aimed for investment banking and corporate jobs, now turning to law as a more secure career choice. Now more than ever, you need to be one step ahead if you are going to outshine people with flawless academic records and a broad array of extra-curricular activities. The good news is it can be done, and this book will show you how.

This book, as the title suggests, tells you how to get a solicitor's training contract at a UK law firm. Given the broad array of firms, and the difficulty of attempting to write a "one size fits all" guide, I have written this book based on my own perspective of working for one of the "magic circle" firms. The magic circle is the name given to the top five law firms in the UK measured by revenue. At the time of writing, these are Clifford Chance LLP, Linklaters LLP, Freshfields Bruckhaus Derringer LLP, Allen and Overy LLP and Slaughter and May LLP. These firms typically seek the best candidates because they work on the biggest transactions for large public companies and so are at the forefront of the transactional market. This book is relevant to all applicants seeking a training contract regardless of the size of the firm, there is just some more specific advice in here as well for the very top firms.

If you have not yet thought of aiming for the top firms, I would suggest you give it some thought for several reasons, some of which I include below. If you are already aiming for the top, feel free to skim this next bit.

- The top UK firms offer the best training and invest a lot of money in you. They hire the best teachers, and push you hard to learn as much as possible during your time with them.

- The work they undertake is of the highest quality as they focus on the most lucrative and hence the most demanding transactions. They claim to offer the most exciting, interesting, challenging and diverse work available to a solicitor.

- They invest a huge amount in graduate recruitment, picking people who are team players and good to work with, so in general the people are good to be around.

- The trainee intakes are large and they are able to sponsor Legal Practice Courses exclusively tailored to their own trainees. This means you make friends in college who start work with you. Amongst over a hundred co-trainees to choose from you are bound to find some kindred spirits.

- The remuneration is good and the whole package generally includes private healthcare, gym membership and many other attractive benefits.

- Their excellent connections with top corporates and banks allow them to offer client secondments to places like Goldman Sachs, J.P. Morgan, the Bank of England and so on. All great to have on your C.V. and will open doors later.

- Finally, they offer international opportunity. While this is not exclusive to magic circle firms, they typically offer the broadest range of overseas secondments. They will pay for language lessons and offer you a free apartment. If you like the idea of working abroad and being paid more to do it, these are the firms for you!

Even if you think the magic circle firms may not be for you, I urge you to read on. The content of this book is relevant to all the big law firms and some sections are relevant to all firms. Whatever training contract you aim for, you want to make sure you get it, so there is no such thing as being over-prepared.

My recent first-hand experience at interview and in the profession will help me give you a great insight into how the system works from the inside out. I have filled the book with hints and tips about how to decide what area of law you are interested in, how to prepare for the application process, the application form and finally how to ace your interview, with sample questions and answers towards the back of the book.

Sound good? Then read on.

Description of the book

"Start where you are"

Christopher Gardner

Whatever stage you are at in life, whether you are still at school, starting university or part way through your degree and are coming to the point where you need to apply for your training contract, this book will help you get where you want to be. If you are at school or starting university, it is not too early to start preparing for your career! You can never start too soon with your preparation, it will save you cramming later.

If you are not sure where you are, and are maybe just thinking about the possibility of being a solicitor, this book will help you gain an understanding of the different stages involved along the common paths to qualification. If you are picking this up just before you are about to submit your application or go to interview for a training contract it is not too late! Read the tips and advice in the later sections of the book, I am convinced it will stand you in good stead.

Structure

So how is the book structured? I have followed the path of my journey, from deciding what type of law and law firm I wanted to work for, through the research and preparation stages for a law conversion course and the legal practice course, to the drafting of an application form and the interview. You do not have to read it cover to cover, rather I suggest you dip in and out depending on what stage you have reached. Or read it all now, so you will know what is coming!

In the first few chapters I will give some background as to the different paths to becoming a solicitor depending on whether you study law or an unrelated subject as your undergraduate degree. Then I will discuss what being a lawyer in an international law firm involves. This should help you get an idea of what the work is actually like in practice and should help you decide if it might be for you. The book will then discuss the application and interview processes with insider knowledge of how to navigate through and land a successful offer. For many hopefuls, the question of how to apply to a big law firm is a complete mystery. I only learned about it through word of mouth and trial and error. It doesn't have to be that way for you as this book will be your guide to the process.

Background on the author

Who am I, and what helps me to tell you how it is? When I wrote this book I was in the final seat of a training contract in a magic circle law firm. I had recently come through the application process and during my time at the firm I assisted in graduate recruitment, giving presentations to open day invitees, undergraduates and law societies. I spoke to a great number of students interested in law, and found that there were a lot of very similar questions. So I thought I would write down the answers and publish them in order to help more people start off on the right foot with their applications and feel more confident about the process by stating it clearly.

What you should get out of this book

This book will help you achieve your goal of securing a training contract with the firm of your choice. It is not a golden ticket, shortcut or cheat sheet. Consider it a guide to the application process, with plenty of hints and tips to help you score highly at each stage. You will have to work hard, but with the help of this book you can target your effort to exactly what is required so that you do not waste time.

By knowing what to expect throughout the application process you can minimize time lost covering irrelevant material. This book will save you time by explaining everything to you so that you do not have to figure it all out for yourself by asking around and researching on the Internet. Finally this book should help you avoid classic mistakes that are easily avoidable that can see candidates passed over. In short, this book will give you your best shot at success!

This book cannot and does not cover everything. I cannot write your applications for you and even if I were to write some model answers they would be of no use to you as they would be quickly spotted as not aligned with your own circumstances. I do provide some ideas for your application form and some sample interview questions and some suggested answers but these are really just to give you an idea and get you thinking, please don't repeat them word for word!

Chapter 2

Paths to law

There are several different paths to a career in law. The main routes follow on from secondary school education with a student's successful completion of his/her A-levels. The first choice is whether to study law as an undergraduate degree or a different, un-related subject such as one of the humanities or a science.

Law undergraduate degree path

- Undergraduate law degree
- LPC
- Training contract

If the student opts for law as an undergraduate course then, whether this is taken as a single subject or combined with another subject such as a language, it will need to be followed by the Legal Practice Course (the "LPC"). The LPC is a post-graduate course that takes from six to nine months to complete, depending on whether it follows the accelerated or traditional model. This course is designed to give future trainee solicitors the background they need to start their training contract and covers a wide range of practical skills, from research to drafting. Once this is complete the student then starts the training contract that takes two years to complete, after which the student becomes a qualified solicitor.

Non-law undergraduate degree path

- Non-law undergraduate degree
- GDL
- LPC
- Training contract

If on the other hand the student studies a non-law subject at university, then he/she will need to complete the Graduate Diploma in Law (the "GDL"). The GDL is designed to teach the student all the necessary parts of a law degree to enable them to work as a solicitor. It is very fast paced and is necessarily high level. It gives a good overall background of the seven major areas of law: Contract, Tort, Criminal, Public, European, Land and Equity. Following successful completion of the GDL, the student then starts the LPC alongside the law undergraduates and their paths are aligned all the way through to qualification.

If you are a non-law undergraduate or graduate and are thinking about a career in law then the GDL allows you to do this. It is very hard work as you are expected to learn a lot in a very short space of time. Someone I studied with described it as like force-feeding your brain. It is very interesting though and despite the pace and quantity of information you are very much spoon-fed everything that you need to know to pass the exams. So you just need to turn up to every lecture and do all the assigned work and you should be okay. It is NOT like another year at university and is much more like being back at school with a classroom environment and small study groups.

As to where to do the GDL or LPC, there are several institutions that offer the course. The most well known and favoured by the magic-circle firms are the College of Law and BPP. Both these colleges have several locations and different fees corresponding to each. For example, in addition to having colleges in Moorgate and Bloomsbury, the College of Law also has a college in York where the fees are lower and the costs of living are more affordable.

It is worth having a look at the different websites to see which may be more suited to you, bearing in mind at this stage that if you secure a training contract with a magic circle firm, they will likely want you to do your GDL at one of their approved institutions. When you get to the LPC your firm may even have a tailored firm-specific course that you will have to do.

Okay, so now you have an idea of the different routes leading to a career as a solicitor, let's get some of the classic insecurities out of the way. If any of the below questions have occurred to you already, or arise during the application process don't worry, you are not alone. Almost everyone who applies worries about the same things but many get hired in spite of them. That is who you need to be. By all means be insecure and afraid of the competition, but don't for a second let it show. Let the other candidates be worrying about you.

Chapter 3

Common questions and insecurities

"Success must be felt within before it can be seen on the outside"

Anon.

I'm not smart enough to be able to work at the top.

If you are studying a degree in a recognised subject (so not football or chocolate) then chances are you have what it takes in mental power. There is a myth that being a lawyer requires you to know the answer to any question in your field, and by extension therefore, to have a fantastic memory and power of recall. As Einstein famously said, "Imagination is more important than knowledge". I would add to that that working as a lawyer is about being able to know where to look to find the answer to a client's question and using your imagination to think of a solution to a problem, rather than learning vast amounts of case law by heart. Research ability is therefore key, and something with which most degrees equip you.

Other skills such as drafting and negotiation are learned on the job. You need to be able to know how to write well, but you don't have to be Dante. In fact it may even serve as a disadvantage if you are a great writer of prose, as this is a field where being clear, concise and to the point is a necessary ability and for some it is difficult to shed the desire to elaborate beyond what is required.

So you need to be able to read, have an idea of where to look for the answers and have an imagination. All very doable!

What academics do I need? Do they only offer positions to people with 1st Class degrees?

There can be no beating about the bush here. Almost all the top firms ask for AAB at A-level and a 2.1 at university. That said, if you did not get (or are not on target to get) that, then all is not lost! If there are extenuating circumstances you will be able to discuss these in your application form. The reality is, that what you get at university is more current than what you got at school. So it is easier to explain away less than stunning A-levels if your university academics are consistently high. They will ask for a full transcript of all the marks you ever got, along with the names of the modules you took. So if you are reading this towards the beginning of your degree it is worth working hard throughout, rather than the "sprint finish" approach favoured by the people of the "first year doesn't count" school of thought. But ultimately it is what you get at the end that really matters so make sure it is a 2.1 or, dare I say it, a First. In a world where almost everyone has a 2.1, if you can get a First then you have taken the first (no pun intended) step to differentiating yourself from your peers.

I didn't go to Oxford or Cambridge or one of the other very highly respected institutions.

Neither did I. It does not matter where you are coming from. What is important is where you are going. More and more top-tier law firms are diversifying their intake so you do not need to be concerned if you did not go to one of the top institutions. The reality is that they still look to the top universities because tradition dictates that the smartest people must go there and therefore by extension that they are the best source of future lawyers. There is an enduring competition between the top firms to get Oxford and Cambridge graduates, so undoubtedly that gives those students an advantage.

However, graduate recruitment teams are desperate for good quality candidates from different universities, and the problem is that there is a real but falsely placed sense of inadequacy from students at other universities that means that they are holding themselves back. I have talked with a lot of students who, before talking to me, weren't even thinking of applying to the magic circle because they thought their university alone would disqualify them. This is a terrible myth. If you know you are good, shout it out loud and let them know who you are.

People can have a presumed advantage over you for all manner of reasons, they went to the right school, they know the right people etc. Some people let the excuse of others being better than them hold them back their whole life. But not you! I know, and you know you are better than that, so let's start by eliminating this fear of the imagined opponent. Whenever you have a moment of insecurity, triggered either by meeting someone who seems amazing or by hearing about him/her, think to yourself, whatever they have done in the past I have more now in the present. However much they claim to want it, I want it more. And because I want it more I will beat them, because I will work harder and I will not rest until I achieve what I set out to achieve. Be the tortoise that comes from behind and overtakes the hare. I know it is possible.

I wasn't the captain of the rugby team or president of the law society. My extra-curricular activities were mainly partying.

It is true that you will be up against some people whose CVs look impossibly well rounded. I know someone with whom I did the Graduate Diploma in Law, who went to Oxford, rowed in their first team, was a competitive kick boxer, spoke three languages, had a lot of relevant work experience, survived on four hours' sleep and on top of it was a very down to earth guy who never bragged about his achievements. (There were more...)

The good news for us mere humans is that there are not very many people like him. Also, the unfortunate reality is that people who are a bit too good, don't tend to be very popular because most people's reaction to them is (as yours may be after reading the description above) to be a bit intimidated. Nobody likes to feel second best (especially hiring partners) and so the faintest whiff of arrogance or self-promotion can result in them being binned.

All graduate recruitment want to see, and the reason they ask for your extra-curricular activities, is that you are able to achieve academically while having a life outside the classroom. Basically that you did not just get your good grades because you spent every waking minute slogging it out in the library. Being a lawyer does require you to be very adaptable and to pick things up quickly and then be able to turn round almost immediately and explain them to a client.

So a balanced student life shows you can do well without it just being a result of hard grind.

Another reason is that they want well-rounded people who can get on with clients, not complete nerds. If your main activity was partying, you can indeed play that up into "good social skills" but you want to think about adding a few more activities, such as a charity run (which required you to organise your training schedule and be self-disciplined enough to stick to it) or talk about your work experience.

I don't know why I want to do law. Money and status are probably the closest reasons I can think of.

This is a question that you are almost guaranteed to be asked on the application form and at interview, so it is best that you get a real answer now before you take things any further. By real I mean one that you believe yourself. It is all very well saying the right thing to an interviewer and managing to convince them that your passion really is corporate law, but ultimately you are going to have to do that job and if deep down you hate the idea of the work, but love the idea of the pay-cheque it might be a good idea to question if this path will really lead to a fulfilled life. You have to want it for the right reasons. Money should not be the first.

If you are studying law, then you will have some idea of what a job in some law firms will involve. However, for commercial, corporate and financial law, you won't really. A law degree is useful background knowledge, but in practice it is the skills that you learn on the LPC and on the job, that you will use day to day. Therefore it is worth finding out what the job entails i.e. what kind of work you will REALLY be doing, not just as a trainee, but also as a junior and senior associate.
It is all very well doing basic and uninteresting work at the beginning (we all have to start somewhere) but if it ultimately

leads to something which is still boring but with more stress then again query if that is really something for you. So look not just to the trainee work but also to that of associates and even partners.

That said a lot of people do really enjoy the work. Working as a lawyer for a large international firm can offer you a variety of challenges that it is difficult to match in any other type of work. In many jobs (such as roles in investment banking, corporates, advertising etc.) you are there to do exactly that, a job. You have a role to fill, whether that is making trades, writing reports on how well a section of a business is performing, selling products or the more mundane administrative tasks that large organisations require people to do in order for them to function.

Working as a lawyer on the other hand requires you to have a certain amount of knowledge but then to be able to use that knowledge in an incredibly adaptable way including running a transaction from an operations perspective and guiding your client through the different stages, advising them of their obligations and steering them away from pitfalls, giving advice on what they can and cannot do and how to best achieve what they want to achieve commercially. It can feel empowering to be advising someone of great stature in the corporate world how best to do something, and to 'add value' by suggesting ways of doing things that have not previously been considered.

Technically you are providing legal services to your client, but in reality you are holding their hand through sometimes very time-pressured and stressful processes where they rely on you to be the calming influence in the storm. There is a steep learning curve, and you will be challenged regularly and forced outside of your comfort zone, but to many (myself included) this is a good thing as you do not have time to get bored. There is no concept of clock watching, waiting for

5.30pm to come around so you can chip off home to your pot noodle and Eastenders.

Each day is dynamic. This uncertainty can be frustrating because you do not know when you will be able to attend social events but at the same time it stops you becoming stale. With technology allowing remote log-in, most firms will be flexible and allow you to work from home when the occasion demands it, so if you have a pressing engagement you will more often than not be able to leave the office and finish up your work later.

I have no idea what being a commercial lawyer entails, how can I know if it is for me?

The long answer is do a lot of research and find out. The short answer is read this book, then decide if you want to continue down the path towards a career in law.

I have heard some scary stories about the hours lawyers work. I have never done anything like that and I am worried that I won't be able to hack it.

The truth is nobody knows when they start how they will stand up to the challenges of this job and people do fare differently. How much you can/want to work is an individual thing. I will say briefly (more later on work practices) that there is a great deal of exaggeration and under-productive working methods in this profession. For some it is a case of bragging rights ("How late were you in last night? Yeah? Well I was in until four!" etc.) For others they take longer to learn, or are less willing to decide that what they have done is satisfactory and so continue to rework material.

There are those who simply don't know any other way than working long hours. That was how they did it at university and that is how they continue at work. Finally there is an internal pressure, created by each round of trainees, that nobody wants to be the one leaving early all the time as it looks like they are not getting any work (because they are bad) or because they fear being seen as shirking their share of the work burden.

Undeniably if you are going to work as part of the legal elite you are going to have to work long hours sometimes. But that doesn't have to be all the time. At the end of the day though you need to be responsible for protecting your own time and making sure you get out when you can. A wise man once said that to do great work you must also learn to be idle. Too many people in this profession think that in order to produce good work you need to be busy all the time. On the contrary, having some down time (read - a life outside the office) is essential for you to come at your work fresh and energised. You will do better as a result. Believe this now, and be prepared to ignore the frightened majority who will tell you otherwise when you start.

When you are required to work hard and late, dive in. Working and studying are very different, and whilst you may feel that you could not study all night, you can work all night. As you would think, things tend to take longer to do and what you produce is rarely your best work (and should probably be checked...) but you will be surprised what you can manage. It is very rare that you will be required to work for sustained periods of time without much sleep and it is usually recognised when you have done so and you are given a chance to recover.

In short, don't let the stories of working hours put you off. They are frequently exaggerated and when it does happen it is not nearly as bad as you imagine.

Quick recap

Hopefully the answers to these questions have helped set you at ease a bit? You don't have to be Einstein, but you do have to have common sense and a willingness to work hard. You don't need to have gone to Oxford or Cambridge (although great if you did!), all you need is the confidence to back yourself against those that did. You don't need to have an extracurricular activities list that reads like a Duke of Edinburgh award, but you do need to present what you have been doing in the right way. You need to have an idea why you want to do law, but not all the reasons. You don't need to have superhuman stamina, but you do have to be prepared to work hard when the occasion demands it. All okay? Are you ready to get stuck in? Now might be a good time for a cup of tea before the next bit...

Chapter 4

What kind of law?

As you will probably already know, there is law about everything. Some areas are more profitable to work in than others. Some are more interesting and can help people. Ideally you want to find something that interests you, but that will remunerate you sufficiently for your time. Mull over the questions below. I suggest you go to your careers library if you are at university, or the town library if you are at school, and do some reading on what the different kinds of law are and what they entail. I set out some brief explanations below.

There are broadly three areas - Advisory / Transactional / Litigious

Advisory involves explaining what a client can and can't do to achieve his objective. He wants to pay less tax? Your job will be to figure out how and explain it to him. Your client needs to sue someone for patent infringement? You tell him what his rights are and how to build a case. Your client wants to merge with another company in a similar field, but is worried that it will create a monopoly? You have to see what has happened before in similar circumstances and advise.

Transactional means getting a deal done. Whether it is that two parties have agreed to merge, or a client who needs to borrow money and a group of banks is willing to lend, you have common intent and you just need to steer them through the process, and importantly ensure that your client's position is protected contractually.

Litigious is where something has gone wrong and your client needs to pursue another company or individual. Or someone is after your client and you need to defend him. Either way, there is no common interest and things can get heated. If you give the wrong advice and your client loses out as a result he may turn on you and sue you.

Which firms specialise in the type of law you want to do?

Get on the Internet and start making a list. Try Chambers Student guides and the Top 100 Legal Employers as well as www.rollonfriday.com and www.lawyer2b.com or www.thelawyer.com as a starting point. The magic circle generally specialise in corporate and financial law, but also have strong litigation departments. Generally the advisory departments are smaller. By way of example, Allen & Overy is primarily focused on finance work and Herbert Smith LLP is known for having a very strong litigation department.

What type of culture are you looking for?

This comes back to the question of what it is that you want. Most UK law firms encourage an atmosphere of teamwork and interdepartmental co-operation. Although not always the case, some think that the American model tends to be more individualistic, with a bonus structure that rewards individuals in line with how much work they have brought into the firm. Where work is shared, credit can be lost. You need to decide for yourself if you want an every man for himself culture or if you want to be more of a team player.

I suggest that you read the insider reports on RollonFriday to get a feel for what the cultures seem to be like. Take whatever you read with a pinch of salt though, as they will be written by one person who may have been having a particularly good or bad day. The accounts of what it is like are by no means representative of a universal experience. The best way to discover the culture though is to go and visit the firms. You can do this by attending an open day or by securing a place on a vacation scheme, or by talking to the graduate recruitment teams at a law fair. I discuss how to do this later in the book.

Do you want to work for a domestic or an international firm? Why?

The distinction here is partly whether you want to be able to work abroad. If you work for a large international firm this will be encouraged. The type of work you do will also reflect the firm's positioning. With international firms you will be involved in multi-jurisdictional transactions with multiple time zones which can affect working practices. All the magic circle firms are international.

What type of work/life balance do you want/will you settle for? Are you prepared to work hard with unpredictable hours, or do you want to have a more predictable 9 – 6pm day?

Not much to say on this really. If you want to earn the big money and work on the big deals you will have to be prepared to work "reactively" i.e. when something kicks off and you are drafted, you drop everything. This is not for everyone. The advantage is that each day can bring a new challenge and you never know quite what is coming. At first this is intimidating but once you learn the ropes it is empowering. You are not just there to do a job, you are required to be able to able to do many different jobs, often learning as you go along.

Quick recap

Whether you think you want to be a transactional, advisory or litigious lawyer the magic circle firms will be able to offer you a taste of each during your training contract to help you decide. If you already have an idea of the kind of work you would like to do, then check which firms focus on this work and target them with your research and applications. As to culture and working environment, this is a personal choice, find out what you can through research and if possible through visiting the different firms and speaking to the people that work there. Whether you want international work or domestic work, it is worth bearing in mind that the magic circle firms are international, but that doesn't mean you have to work abroad if you don't want to. Finally, everyone wants a good work/life balance. Working for a magic circle firm does not mean that you cannot have one. Provided you are prepared to work when they need you to, you will find they are much more flexible when things are not busy.

Still on board? Then let's press on.

Chapter 5

What do you want and how much do you want it?

"Success consists of going from failure to failure without loss of enthusiasm"

Winston Churchill

Before going any further you need to ask yourself that fundamental question. What do you want and how much do you want it? Put the kettle on, sit down and really think about it. What is it that you want out of this? What do you think that a career in commercial law will offer you? If you are asked this at interview you may well answer differently to the following more honest reasons taken from some people I interviewed which seem to be primarily that of money and status. I will elaborate.

Money - You have worked hard to get where you are and you are likely going to work hard for the next 35 – 40 years of your life, so you may as well get paid for it right?

Status – You want your friends to be impressed and your enemies to fear you. You want members of the opposite sex (or the same, whatever) to swoon when you tell them who you work for and what you do. Your parents may have helped you with the costs of your tuition and you want to make them proud so they can tell their friends that you work for x law firm which is x largest in the UK or something.

If these are your first responses you are not alone, and a career in law might still be fine. However I would say that you might want to dig a little deeper. You will need to do this job for potentially a long time, so you would be well advised to find out what exactly it involves and if you think you would like doing that. Money and status should not be your primary reasons for doing this. You need something more.

Other responses are that law offers an exciting opportunity to work with like-minded individuals at the top of their game on market-leading transactions set within a global context. That working as a lawyer enables you to influence a client's decisions at the formative stage of transactions rather than just executing his instructions. Your opinion on matters will be sought by people at the top of their field, whom you would normally read about in the newspaper, because they value your advice and perspective.

For intelligent people such as yourselves money is not enough as a motivational factor. Law offers you a chance to be challenged on a daily basis and pushed outside of your comfort zone forcing you to tap into your inner reserve of determined resourcefulness. It is one of a few jobs where you can leave the office after a hard day and think "Wow I can't believe I did that". It can be really exciting and when you overcome a seemingly insurmountable problem you feel really good about yourself.

But, be warned, it is also hard. Really hard. You need to be prepared for that now or else go home. It is hard because of the speed at which you will be required to learn and adapt once you arrive. It is hard because you will be expected to handle workloads and responsibility that you are not ready for, but that you are told to "run with". You will be expected to act like you know what is going on in situations where you have no idea what is going on or even who the people are that you are dealing with. You will need to be the oasis of calm in the eye of the storm despite all this. You will see the whole spectrum of human emotion, from crushing failure, dash to the toilet panic, to satisfied elation when a deal is signed. You will work harder than you have ever worked in your life. But you will achieve things greater than you have achieved so far. This is worth fighting for, but you have to be ready to fight. As some Americans say, "you gotta come ready to play".

If you only want this for money, you will not want is as much as someone who wants it because they are really interested in global transactions, or high level litigation. They will make the interviewer believe they want it, because they are not acting. They really do want it. Remember that it costs between £150,000 and £250,000 to train a solicitor in the top UK firms. You have to be a good investment for them. The more you want it now, the more likely you are to stick with it when the going gets tough.

Okay so you want it, but how much do you want it? Because most people just kind of want it. They want it because they need a job post-university and think this is probably a good fit. But they don't really want it that badly. They don't want it more than they want to watch their favourite programme on television, or more than going on a night out with their friends. Do you want it enough to say no when a friend or roommate tells you they are going on a night out and that if you don't come you are no fun?

To illustrate this point, there is an old story about a man who goes to see a successful businessman and asks him the secret to success. The businessman tells him to meet him the following morning down by the ocean. The next day at dawn, the businessman walks out into the ocean with the man. Once they are in up to their chests he grabs the man's head and holds it under the water. Just before the man is about to pass out, he pulls the gasping man up and says "How much do you want to breathe right now? If you really want to succeed, you need to want it as much as you want to breathe right now".

When you are drowning, you are not thinking about what you are going to wear on your next night out, or what is on television right then. You are not thinking if you should make a move on that girl in your class or if you should wait till the next party. All you are thinking is how much you want to breathe. You need to think of your will to succeed in the same light. You want nothing more and will not stop until you get what you want. You have focus.

Have I put you off yet or are you hungry for more? If you think that you want to enter this world then read on. I will do my best to arm you with the necessary tools based on my experience working with graduate recruitment and human resources and from having recently come through the process myself. It is not impossible by any means, and if you avoid a few common pitfalls and present yourself in the right way then you will be well on your way to that desk of glory.

Chapter 6

Believe

"I know you all doubt me, but I'm gonna show YOU, how great I am"

Muhammad Ali

"He who says he can and he who says he cannot are both usually right"

Confucius

This book will discuss detailed advice on progressing from research to application form to interview then to job. Underpinning all of the following sections is a state of mind that must drive your every thought, action and response. That state of mind is a drive to succeed, founded on a strong self-belief that success is coming to you.

Self-belief and motivation are two things that cannot be bought or cleverly created with a deft twist of words. If you do not believe that you are capable of succeeding at interview you will fail. If you do not believe that you are capable of standing shoulder to shoulder with those that are already doing the job then you will fail. Believing that you have already won the job and that the interview is just a formality (which arguably in some ways it is) is vital to your success.

How to develop self-belief in face of stories of an insurmountable challenge

Okay so you understand it is important, but how do you create self-belief when you have almost no idea what it is that you will be doing if you are awarded a training contract and have already heard all the horror stories of how much stamina you need to have to survive, how smart you need to be, how personable you need to be and so on? If you are initially thinking that you probably don't have what it takes, you are in the majority. But there is good news, I will show you why you do have what it takes.

Confidence at interview, as in all things in life, is built on a belief based on experience that you are going to be good at what you do. Psychologists term this "high self-efficacy". The key is to research and experience as much as possible that is related to the job you are going for, as this will enable you to believe and confidently say that you are right for the job and demonstrate why with examples.

So let's start at the beginning. Remember I said that this would take work? Well roll your sleeves up, because we start now.

Your own research

You would not start to write an essay before doing the research. If you have tried this (I certainly have) you find that you don't know where to start, the few ounces of knowledge you can scrape together don't gel together well, you suffer from writer's block and you end up feeling frustrated and ultimately not doing well. Compare this with sitting down to write when you have already read most of the books on the subject. Your thoughts are overflowing, a quick sketch plan is all it takes and the words are pouring out.

This is what you want to be feeling like on interview day. The good news is I can tell you exactly where to look to get the knowledge you need. The bad news is that there are no short-cuts here. This is where you will pass or fail the interview. Without over-egging the Muhammad Ali quotes, he once famously said:

"The fight is won or lost far away from witnesses - behind the lines, in the gym, and out there on the road, long before I dance under those lights".

The same applies to you. The financial press will become your training ground.

In addition to reading, as soon as possible get out there and start accumulating relevant work experience. This is your most vital asset as it demonstrates many key skills that are going to be relevant to your profession – real interest, initiative, confidence and drive. I will discuss how to get this work experience later in the book.

Who are you and what have you been doing all these years?

Dig deep people. What is it that you feel confident about? Write a list now. What is it that you feel you are good at, and what do you feel that you are not so good at. By way of example your list might include some of the following (popular comments from people I have spoken to):

Good – I am good with people, love to socialise and am good at maintaining a friendship group. I am responsible and people trust me with their secrets and to be there when they need me. I work hard and take a lot of care over my work, always making sure that an essay is 100% right before I submit it to a lecturer for review.

Bad – I am not captain of a sports team, and have hardly any real life experience. I feel awkward around people I don't know at first and often worry afterwards if I have said the right thing. I am not sure that my socializing at university will transfer well to socializing with colleagues I don't know or with clients who are much older than me and with whom I have nothing in common.

This is not meant to be a formal list, so just write what you really feel are your strengths and weaknesses, not what you think you would say in response to this question. Be honest with yourself so that you can fully address your weaknesses before interview. If you are really brave you could ask others what they think your strengths and weaknesses are, although be prepared to hear some things that you may not like!

This is important as you first need to understand yourself what it is you think you have to offer, before you can identify the areas you need to work on. This exercise will help to build your self-confidence as you show yourself that you do have attributes that would be very desirable to an employer.

I will discuss tips on how to research and get work experience later, but for now, understand that a combination of these three areas, research, work experience and self-understanding will help you understand what it is that you are going for, and will increase your self-belief that you are capable of getting it.

Next then, we start with how to get an understanding of your goal. Without understanding exactly what your target is, how can you expect to hit it?

Chapter 7

Preparation – how to get where you want to be

"If I was given six hours to chop down a tree, I would spend the first four hours sharpening the axe"

Abraham Lincoln

Before we delve into what you need to do to understand what you are aiming for, and how to prepare, a word about organisation. As you already have very busy schedules, it is important to keep track of the important dates that will have an impact on your application. These are dates not just relating to when you need to submit applications but also of when there are opportunities to meet representatives of the law firms.

I will describe more about the various events later, but for now the key events are the summer vacation schemes, the winter vacation schemes, the law fairs and the open days. The summer vacation scheme traditionally used to be for law undergraduates only, to be completed in their penultimate year and last four weeks. Now more firms are opening this up to non-law undergraduates as well. The scheme is typically four weeks in the summer and is designed to give a structured insight into the firm, with students spending time in one or more departments, trying their hand at real work.

The winter vacation schemes are traditionally shorter (two weeks) and are for final year non-law students. The principal is the same as the summer schemes, only the timescale is different. Law fairs are held on university campuses and consist of lots of stalls, each one set up by a different law firm. It is an opportunity for students to meet the graduate recruitment teams and current trainees and ask questions.

Open days are usually by invitation only, following a successful application by a student. They are an opportunity to visit the offices of a firm, meet the people that work there and listen to various presentations on the firm.

All these events take place in one academic year, and so if you are following three to five firms there are lots of dates to keep track of! My method was to use a table, with the names of the law firms down the left side and the different schemes along the top. If you have a calendar on your computer using a program like Microsoft Office or Apple's calendar then you can set alarms that will tell you when a deadline is approaching so you can make sure you have done everything you need to do.

You can get dates for the different events from each firm's graduate recruitment website, or your university law society for information on law fair dates.

Once you know when your various deadlines are you can begin your research. There are two key areas you need to focus your research on. The law firm and the wider market context and then how they interact. First I will discuss how to broaden and develop your commercial awareness; second, how to target specific law firms and get to know how they tick.

Commercial awareness

Commercial awareness is a term you will come across with increasing frequency. Just what does that mean? It is something that you will be expected to be very good at, and yet until you meet people in this world, it is difficult to get a clear explanation of just what it is. Allow me to assist.

In essence what graduate recruitment want (because ultimately this is what it comes down to) is evidence that you understand the commercial market. In reality, there is no such thing as a commercial market place per se. All there is, is a web of entities joined together by economic relationships. These entities are banks and borrowers, traders and suppliers, distributors and buyers. Governments also play a role, but don't worry too much about that for now.

So who are the big corporates and banks? What makes them tick? How have they been affected by recent global political and economic issues? What is their position in the big picture, who are their suppliers and clients?

The key here is to be able to demonstrate to graduate recruitment that you have an idea of what is going on with that law firm's clients. At this high level, clients expect much more than just legal knowledge. That you have a good understanding of the legal issues is taken as a given, what clients really want is to know how they can best operate their business, or carry out a transaction in a legal and tax-effective way. So in order to best advise them you need to know what motivates them now, how they run a successful business and their goals for the future.

How do you do this? Subscribe to the Financial Times ("FT") and to the Economist as soon as possible. Right now in fact, I can wait. I prefer the Economist as it is generally written in an interesting and accessible style without too much industry-specific terminology. The FT cannot be beaten though on its up-to-the-minute reporting. So both should be used together.

Be warned, for most people the best initial intent is often easily thwarted. A common experience is that someone goes and buys the FT on a Saturday morning full of a will to succeed, sits down to read it and then finds that they don't really understand what any of it is about. This naturally leads to frustration, boredom and distraction and then setting the paper aside with a mental note to return to it later. This is because when you start reading you will come across a lot of unfamiliar terms that are bandied about freely, that can make an article impenetrable.

Understanding the commercial and financial world is quite like learning a new language. When you start you will likely find references to concepts that you are not familiar with and abbreviations that are completely alien (e.g. CDOs – Collateralised Debt Obligations or CDSs – Credit Default Swaps) along with a host of jargon like 'poison pill' and 'white knight' and the like. Initially, you will not be able to pick it up and skim read it and absorb all the important details of the latest deals before (or during) your morning jog.

This is where the graft comes in. You need a highlighter and a notebook. Pick an article that is big news and read it thoroughly. Set yourself 15 minutes to read it. Pore over it and highlight any words you don't COMPLETELY know the meaning of. Shares, bonds, securities, receivables, securitisations, collateralised debt obligations, FTSE etc. Do you really know what a share is? Could you write me a definition or explain it to me in an interview? What is LIBOR? Do you know the difference between a share and a bond? What is a management buyout? Or a takeover as opposed to an acquisition?

Anything that you don't know, look it up. Google is a fantastic starting place, as there are all manner of financial dictionaries out there that will explain it to you. Then write down in your own words what you think it means in your notebook. Using your own words is a vital mental process to comprehension, and later, for recall. Make a note of what it is you don't understand and later look up and jot down the definition.

Build up a reference notebook of terms and their definitions. Often a small word or abbreviation can actually refer to a very complex concept that requires a lot of thinking about, multiple explanations and diagrammatic representation. It is important that you invest the time understanding these. Consider investing in a financial dictionary. After a while you will start to see more and more terms that you are familiar with and the articles will become much more accessible.

If you buy one FT and study one article an evening for a week, which needn't take more than 15-30 minutes a day, you will soon notice a drastic improvement in your comprehension. Think of it as learning a new language, except that you already have the grammatical structure and joining words. What you lack is vocabulary. So start making your list and get learning. Make this a task for this weekend – notebook, highlighter, FT. Buy.

The better you get the less time you will need to take 'studying' an article and the more time you can spend just reading it. Then you can start grouping articles around a similar subject. Start a ring-bound file. Cut out articles that relate to similar subject matter and keep them together in a plastic insert in the file. You will start to build up an in-depth understanding of the issue or deal at hand and its impact on the wider market.

When you come to writing your application form and the question that asks you to discuss a recent commercial event or issue that has interested you, you will have a whole file of research on different issues to draw upon. Then it is just a case of summarising the parts that you found interesting into 200 words or thereabouts for your application form, which you can then easily expand upon at interview.

The other great source of market information is the Economist. As it is published weekly it has already summarised the key issues and selected the best bits, so it is saving you some of the leg-work.

If folders are not your thing, another way of doing it, if you are more visually orientated, is to buy some blue tack and go to town on your wall. I did this, cutting out articles from the Economist, highlighting the interesting bits and sticking it on my wall above my desk (careful not to go too overboard though lest your friends try to have you sectioned). That visibility of the articles meant that in idle moments when I was studying, my eyes would wander over the text on the wall. So the information was absorbed more by osmosis than by applied study. It was also a nice break from studying (although not quite as nice as watching TV or say, a lot of other things).

Quick recap

Does all that make sense? Study that FT, make a note of any terminology you wouldn't feel happy explaining in an interview and learn it. Your goal is to become comfortable enough with what they are talking about that you don't need to study the articles any more, you can just pick up a copy of the FT and read. Build your folder, or cover your wall in articles, whatever works for you. Next we target the law firms individually.

Firm-specific research

As soon as possible start researching the background of the firms you are going to be targeting so that you are comfortable in the following areas:

- What type of law do they specialise in?

- Who are their key clients and what do they do?

- What big deals or litigation have they recently been involved in that the press is talking about?

- How does their firm fit into the wider context of law firms and a commercial background?

- What is their current strategy and plan for the future? Are they planning any mergers with overseas firms (think Australia, Hong Kong, Brazil)?

- What are their core values?

Where should you be looking to find this information?

Careers library

Your first port of call should be your careers library if you are at university. Speak to your careers advisor and ask him to point you in the direction of the Chambers Student guide. This lists all the law firms and what they do.

The Internet

The firms' websites are gold mines and yet are often overlooked. You will find that they will usually tell you an enormous amount about themselves (it is in their interest that you are well informed). Check the graduate recruitment site for their core values, what they are most proud of in terms of work they have done and for their trainee accounts of what it is like working there. I know one firm has a description of what a deal process typically involves and the role of a trainee.

Roll on Friday (www.rollonfriday.com) claims to tell it how it really is. This is an unaffiliated website that is built upon the anonymous contributions of people working for the firms. So you will see the good, the bad and the ugly. Take it all with a pinch of salt (as anonymous is also unverified) but it gives a good alternative to the official material.

The Lawyer (www.thelawyer.com) and the Lawyer2b (www.lawyer2b.com) give some good articles on what the different firms are doing and news specific to the legal market.

Check the FT and the Economist by searching their websites for any articles that discuss the firm.

Law fairs

This is your first opportunity to meet the people that really work there. Go to law fairs armed with which firms you want to speak to and have some intelligent questions to ask them that are not just "what are the hours like?" There will be people there from graduate recruitment. Make sure you speak to them and, more importantly, that they remember you.

Tip: Use a hook to jog their memory later. Tell them an

interesting fact about yourself that is memorable and when you follow up with them mention that fact. E.g. I was the girl from Lithuania or I was the guy who fell into your stand. Don't: Just hoover up the freebies and not talk to anyone. The best freebies rarely correlate with the best law firm.

Your network

Speak to anyone you know that works at your targeted firm or at similar places, most people can find a tenuous link to a lawyer! Using this tactic allows you to find out off the record what it is actually like to work as a lawyer. You can ask your more basic questions without fear of judgment.

The next thing you need to do is experience first-hand what it is you claim to be so interested in. Actions speak louder than words and having been there and done it will show the interviewer (as well as you) that you know what you are talking about and will add conviction to your answers at interview.

Chapter 8

Work experience

"You know more of a road by having travelled it than by all the conjectures and descriptions in the world"

William Hazlitt

I have already mentioned how important it is to add a range of work experience to your portfolio. Academic results will suffice only to tick one box on an application form reviewer's checklist. You need to show that you want this job because you have relevant work experience that you have done of your own volition and enjoyed - so you know that this is the job for you. Your competition will have it, you need it too.

I hesitate to say anything will do, but anything is better than nothing, and if you are smart you can turn the most unrelated job into a fine display of your relevant skill set. For example, a successful candidate worked as a barman on a university year abroad and used that as an example of taking the initiative in a foreign environment, balancing work with study (time management), handling money under pressure (reliability), all in another language.

Obviously though, a job in the legal field will help you even more when it comes to demonstrating your interest in law. Depending on what stage you are at you may be considering either applying for a formal vacation scheme with a large firm, or an ad-hoc self-created work experience with a high street firm.

Vacation schemes

Vacation schemes are programmes run by the big law firms that can run in either the summer or the winter, for between one and four weeks and are designed to be a structured introduction to real working life inside a large law firm. The schedules usually involve spending some time in more than one department and there are lots of social activities organised, with the aim of getting all the vacation schemers to interact outside of the workplace. In short they are great fun, but they also usually offer you an interview for a training contract. So they are also a great way in.

Be warned, they are more competitive than the training contracts. There are only 40 vacation scheme places in comparison with over 100 training contract places, and the same number of candidates apply for both! The application process is usually similar to that for the training contract, so I will not go into it here. In short there is an application form and an interview.

I cannot stress how good getting a placement on a vacation scheme is. It means that they definitely think you have what it takes. Then you have to endure what is essentially a 3-4 weeks' assessment, the culmination of which is the interview. Provided you work hard and impress during those few weeks though, you are in a very strong position to get an offer for a training contract. So definitely put these deadlines in your calendar and apply.

If you don't get an offer for a vacation scheme, don't be disheartened. Because of the numbers involved most don't. Consider it great practice, follow up with graduate recruitment to find out what you need to tweak in your application and apply for the training contract.

But that much is pretty obvious. What will make you stand out is the next step, and ties in again with not giving up. This part is absolutely essential if you do not get a vacation scheme, but is also very desirable even if you do. I am talking about ad-hoc work experience. So many think it is not possible, but it absolutely is. How do you make your own work experience? Read on.

Ad-hoc work experience with high street firms

Time to get pro-active and create your own opportunities.

In the first instance draw on any contacts that you have. Whether they are friends of the family, of neighbours or of your friends' parents, or even if it is through your university careers service (who may still be in touch with past students who now work as lawyers). Put the word out that you are very keen to find any work experience you can. Even if it is only a couple of days.

If this fails then it is time to do it the traditional way. By mailshot. Write letters to every law firm that you would be prepared to travel to for work experience. For me this was all those in my home town outside of London. All the small high street firms that deal with conveyancing, divorces and the like. The smaller the better, because you will get a chance to really see the whole process of law in practice and maybe even go to court. These letters will most likely be ignored and put on a pile of papers to be looked at never. So don't expect the phone to start ringing like crazy. Most people would give up at this stage and try elsewhere, or just give up. Not you!

This next part is vital. Follow up the letter with a call after three business days or so. Introduce yourself, say you wrote them a letter and that you are following up to check if there was anything else that they might need to know. What you are really doing though is telling them who you are and that you are looking for the opportunity to shadow one of the partners for a few days. Most small offices never get work experience students in and the partners may be more than happy to have some eager person asking for their guidance and advice.

Now don't be surprised if you get fobbed off by the secretary, or told that whoever the partner is will call and he/she doesn't. Call back. They have busy lives (probably) and you will not even be on their list of things to do, so you are really trying to catch them at a good moment and appeal to their good nature. They were here once too.

When you do get through you have a very short time to establish a common ground so you get on with them. Cast your net wide, saying what school you went to, what gym you go to etc. If you are from the same town doubtless you can find something in common.

A successful candidate told me about a story involving spinning. Although this is not a perfect example as he did not actually have it in common with the partner. For the unfamiliar great, spinning is a class you take at the gym with a lot of exercise bikes with adjustable difficulty lined up in rows facing an instructor. You all pedal frantically together to techno music, while the instructor tells you when to sprint, when to up the difficulty to simulate a hill climb, when to feign a heart attack etc.

The candidate told the partner that he went to the gym a lot and the partner said he did too, and had he ever done a spinning class? HAD he?! Well no. But he wasn't going to let on. So he said that he loved spinning. The partner offered him three weeks' work experience on condition that he went to a spinning class with him. How hard could it be, right?

As it turned out the spinning class was an advanced class, and the instructor announced at the beginning that they would be doing the Tour de France "a hill section". So it was astonishingly hard. Apparently he saw spots at the end and felt 'unusual'. But he did it. Later that week, as part of the work experience he went to a trial at a county court, and off the back of meeting the barrister there, and the partner's recommendation, he was offered a mini-pupillage at a London Chambers.

Quick recap

Do whatever it takes to get work experience. (Almost) nothing is below you and you must not accept no as an answer. Be proactive and create your own opportunities. Next, your biggest asset. A precision instrument honed to perfection and ready to be displayed in all its glory. It's time to break out that personality you've been working on all these years.

Chapter 9

You, glorious you

"Our deepest fear is not that we are inadequate, but that we are powerful beyond measure"

Nelson Mandela

In addition to researching the market and the specific law firms (their partners, the deals they have done and so on) you also need to be able to describe things that you have done in life that demonstrate your personal qualities, such as problem solving ability, leadership and capacity to work to a tight deadline. Work experience examples are ideal but don't forget to use illustrations from your personal life too.

For instance, a successful candidate told a story at interview that was from an Erasmus year abroad. She had booked accommodation in the university halls, filled in the exhaustive documentation, supplied all necessary passport copies and birth certificate and was good to go. However, on arrival she was told they had lost her documentation and had already allocated all the rooms. There was nothing left and she had to look elsewhere. Only there was nothing left elsewhere either. Anyone who was organised had sorted out their accommodation months before. It was a wasteland.

She managed to get someone from the Erasmus program to help her find a place, then had to negotiate with the landlady to get her to accept a substitute for the role of a French guarantor, which is usually the parents of the tenant. This involved extensive negotiation with a bank and creative thinking to get money transferred from the UK, all under serious time pressure of 48 hours (which was as long as the landlady would hold the apartment for her).

This example, as you may see, demonstrates some skills that would be relevant to a legal profession. This candidate doesn't need to say "I am good at problem solving under pressure in an international context" because what could be better evidence of that than being homeless negotiating a lease in a foreign language with an inflexible landlady? The key here is to provide examples that speak for themselves.

You will doubtless have similar stories of challenges you have faced in life and how you have overcome them. Another great one I heard, was of an Australian guy who got an offer to study at Oxford, but could not afford the staggering tuition fees of £30+ thousand a year. He worked full time up until he was due to leave to start the academic year but had only managed to save half of what he needed. Many would have given up. Not him, he went anyway and started the year backing himself that he would find a scholarship whilst he was there that would pay the remaining fees. And you know what, he did.

Quick Recap

Think how your stories of personal struggle can be used to show the skills you will be required to demonstrate as a lawyer. Think problem solving, negotiation, team work, drive and a will to succeed in the face of overwhelming odds.

Got it? Okay, we have covered a lot up to now, and you should have much to think about. Now would be a good time to pause and digest, because next I will look at the application process, starting with the application forms.

Chapter 10

Application forms

"A man's accomplishments in life are the cumulative effect of his attention to detail"

John Foster Dulles

This is the first stage of the formal application process. By now you should have done your preliminary research and decided on a select few law firms that you are going to apply to. Sleeves still rolled up? Good.

So what is the application form? Quite simple really, an online series of question and answer boxes often with word count limiters. The questions are designed to be as open as possible to give you an opportunity to demonstrate who you are and what you have achieved to date. It is designed to be fairer to all applicants than a simple CV and cover letter. Although more arduous for both the applicant and reviewer, the structured questions at least put everyone on the same footing. You know what information is required of you and it is up to you how well you present your answers.

It is important to note that they take a long time to do well. Some people say they can knock one out in a few hours, I would say that you need to set aside at least ten hours for the first drafting and about five hours to check it (ignore any time suggestions on the form of ten minutes or so for a section). Really you should take as long as you can realistically afford (bearing in mind your other academic commitments). Research is key, but you will only really need to do a lot of research for a few of the sections (e.g. the commercial knowledge section). The rest will be about you and your interest in law, which just requires some thought.

The time you take to check it is vital. If you have friends or loved ones that you are willing to ask (and who are willing to answer) to help with your review all the better. It needs to be absolutely 100% perfect in terms of spelling and punctuation. A single mistake, no matter how slight (pay attention to those apostrophes!) will result in your application being politely binned.

This is because graduate recruitment's job is to select the best candidates they can find. How good they appear to be at their job to those that matter will depend largely on the quality of the candidates that they put in front of the partners. If you look bad, they look bad by extension. They will need to put your application form in front of a partner and, as they are not allowed to edit them, what they receive must go to the partner in its original form.

So do not do yourself the obvious disservice of spending two days researching and crafting the best application form in history, only to fall down at the last and simplest hurdle. I don't know the exact statistics, but I have it on good authority and have seen for myself that a staggering number of forms have very basic errors that a diligent proof read would have picked up. So leave it a day, print it out and go back to it with fresh eyes, or even better do this in combination with a third party reviewer, preferably a relation as they will feel morally obligated to help out and will not pull any punches with their scathing criticism.

How many you should apply to is up to you. Some take the scattergun approach and go for as many as possible, with the logic that this will increase their chances of a successful hit. Some focus on only two or three. Whilst there is no right or wrong approach, it is important to stress the importance of treating each application uniquely.

Many of the application forms contain similar questions worded slightly differently (yes, surprisingly, graduate recruitment teams do look at the competition...) and so there is an obvious temptation to cut and paste with some minor adjustments. Do not do this. Graduate recruitment can spot a cut and paste job a mile off, and even if they don't, an adapted copy and paste application will not stand up to one that someone has tailored from scratch to that particular law firm. If it's worth doing...

Each application as previously mentioned will take a long time to complete, as cutting corners is not an option. If you are including the time that it takes to research it as well, then you are looking at weeks rather than hours. Think of it as another module of your degree and treat it with the same (if not more) importance you would an assessed module. All this will have a limiting effect on how many applications you choose to do.

The ideal number is said to be five, according to various different graduate recruitment teams. I only did three. Obviously it would be unwise to invest all your time in one, in case you don't fit what that firm is looking for. You can of course do as many as you feel comfortable doing well, but as soon as you feel yourself cutting corners, stop.

Writing tips for the form – things to think about

What are the typical sections?

- Education – what school you went to and the results you got there.

- Qualifications – what have you achieved so far in life?

- Degree subject, module titles and results (Remember when they said enjoy your first year because it doesn't count? Ah.)

- Language skills – anything more than English?

- Work experience – where you have done it, how long for and the type of work you did.

- Application questions - the big ones and will be the ones that you will need to think about the most. Example question areas are:

- Why commercial law?
- Your extra-curricular activities
- What would you bring to the firm?
- Describe a commercial issue that interests you
- Any extenuating circumstances that affected your grades
- Diversity – what is your ethnic background?

What is the goal?

To get to interview by convincing your reader/reviewer that you are a worthy candidate that will make them look good if they put you forward in front of a partner. To stand out against the crowd.

Who are you writing for?

Someone who is experienced at reviewing these forms and has a lot to look at. Stand out quickly, make your positive points shine out clearly and easily.

This comes back to the point above. Use clear simple language that is well structured. Read the Economist and note how important structure is to their articles. It should be formal English, but not flowery prose. Must above all be accessible and use everyday language with nothing fancy thrown in. Ask yourself, what is more impressive, someone who can explain a complex concept in complex language or someone who can explain a complex concept in simple language?

Keep the structure the same as a mini essay. The first sentence should answer the question, the next few sentences should back up your answer with evidence, and the last couple of sentences should summarise and conclude.

How to address negatives?

This is most appropriate for your extenuating circumstances section. If you have some bad grades, say why. Make sure you have a good reason. It is important to be clear and upfront. Make sure you turn them into a positive. For example: my grades weren't so good that semester because I was so focused on fundraising for my charity hike up Everest.

Length of responses?

This is usually limited by the form, otherwise try not to exceed 200-250 words per answer.

Once you have drafted your answers, printed them out, checked them and sent them to someone else to check them, then you are ready to submit. The more time you can allow yourself to check them the better. Leave it a day or two and come back with a fresh perspective.

Remember to use the table I described in Chapter 7 (or something similar of your own creation) to keep on top of deadlines for submission and set a calendar alarm to follow up with graduate recruitment to check that they have received your form. If you don't receive a confirmatory email soon after submitting, then you need to pick up the phone. This could be the first stage of putting a voice to a name and letting them know how keen you are.

A successful candidate told me that he had submitted his application form for a vacation scheme and yet heard nothing from graduate recruitment by way of confirmation of receipt of his form. He kept calling to ask if they had received his form and they kept assuring him that they had, but that they had been busy with other work and so had not got to reviewing it yet. As the dates when the interviews were due to take place approached and the candidate still had not heard anything, he gave one last call asking graduate recruitment if they were sure they had received his form.

It then turned out that they had not received it, but that it was stuck in the system, saved but not submitted. Graduate recruitment then reviewed it and, apologising that the vacation scheme places had already all been awarded, invited him to an open day.
He used the open day to meet as many people who worked at the firm as possible and particularly to meet with graduate recruitment to discuss his form and what could be done to improve it so that it was the best it could be for the training contract application. All of this really helped him get a

training contract and would not have come about if he had not had the confidence to pick up the phone.

Quick recap

Aim to do about three to five forms. Spend a long time researching each firm and finding out what it is that they are after. Take your time over the drafting and take even longer over the checking. Ask for help with the review and make absolutely sure that if you fail it will not be because of presentation or typos. Finally, make sure you chase graduate recruitment if you don't hear from them, it may make the difference between success and failure.

Be confident that you will get to interview but if for whatever reason you are told that they are sorry but they cannot take your application further, then it is time to move to the next section.

Chapter 11

How to deal with rejection

"Defeat only becomes failure when you accept it as such"

Anon.

At some stage in your application process you will face rejection. It is almost an inevitable part of this process. As mentioned in the application section you will probably be applying to between three and five law firms, all of which will have a different idea of working practices and culture and the type of the person that they want to recruit. It is possible, but not likely, that you will receive offers from everyone you apply to. It is much more likely that you will not be a perfect fit for all of them and you will be rejected by some.

It is unfortunate that the way the system works, those firms that decide you are not for them will send their rejection letters far faster than those who have decided to make you a positive offer. So you may get a flurry of rejection letters. It is obviously discouraging.

Most applicants face some rejection, what is important is how you handle it. Follow up with the graduate recruitment team(s) that rejected you. You can be rejected for any number of reasons, the most common of which is spelling and punctuation on your form or cover letter. They will have thousands of applications that they have to reject, so it is up to you to take the initiative and pick up the phone and call them to find out what it is that you need to improve.

- Say that you were very disappointed not to have been invited to interview because they are the one law firm you really wanted. However, you understand the number of candidates that apply and that they have to draw the line somewhere.

- Ask what exactly you need to do to get your form up to scratch. What specific section?

- If you were to improve that section and apply again would you be in with a chance?

- If you simply haven't got enough experience or your grades aren't high enough then tell them that you will go and improve on that and apply again next time, and ask them to watch out for your form.

- What else can you do to show them how keen you are?

The key here is to make them aware of exactly who you are, how disappointed you are to have failed to make the grade, to find out what you need to tweak and to let them know that you will be applying again and to look out for your form. Graduate recruitment teams are inundated with written applications, but hardly anyone ever calls them to talk about their application, especially after rejection. You will be immediately putting a voice and personality to the name and this will help enormously when you re-apply. The goal is to get the graduate recruitment person on your side so they want to put your form in front of a partner.

I cannot possibly stress enough the importance of picking up the phone. For many people, asking why they have been rejected is difficult because they fear that the other person might laugh at them or tell them they fundamentally don't have what it takes. This will not happen. Also, the way I see it, you already have nothing. If you call them and don't learn anything useful, what have you lost?

If you have gone about your application in a way that I have suggested in this book the recruiters should already know who you are, so this should make the follow-up call easier.

Above all, getting it wrong is a necessary part of success. Embrace it, learn from it and move on. Remember, how much you want it? Don't give up.

Quick recap

If you don't get the offer you want, then it is time to find out why. Learn what you can and try again. Make sure they hear how keen you are and that you will do whatever it takes to show them that on paper.

Okay, let's assume now that you have at least one offer for an interview. The next section deals with how to prepare before the interview with some sample questions to be thinking about, how to prepare on the day and lots of tips on how to act during the interview to make sure that you put your best self forward.

Chapter 12

Interview preparation

"Fix up, look sharp"

Dizzee Rascal

"Remember, who you are is a very fluid concept"

Will Smith as Hitch

Great news! You got an interview. Give yourself a pat on the back. But the tournament is not over. You have earned a place in the final, now you need to play your best game ever.

Dress to impress

For all but the privileged few students, designer clothes are a luxury that can easily be dispensed with for beer money. At university most people dress in what could be described as the bare minimum of socially acceptable attire, with more than one pyjama appearance at my university lectures. That (obviously) has to change when you go to your interview.

This is one of those few opportunities in life when you can buy something as expensive as possible without feeling guilty. See this as an investment in yourself. You need to set a budget for the maximum you can afford and then stick to it. You still need to eat.

Your goal is to look like you already work at the firm which is interviewing you. Interviewers are subjective creatures and their first impression (made in the first two seconds of meeting you) will, unless something terrible happens, be built around how you look.

If it looks like you are already a trainee of the type they are used to dealing with they can more easily picture hiring you. If they think you look like you slept in your suit or that you borrowed your dad's (or mum's) you have unnecessarily created a barrier to your employment.

Stay conventional. This is not a time for you to try and look like some A-lister who wants to be different. If you are a natural non-conformist in life, at interview you need to blend in (you might also want to question how happy you would be conforming every day of your life). This is not an opportunity to make any statement other than 'I belong'. You want to look and feel like Bruce Wayne, not the Joker.

For both girls and boys this means wearing a suit. Pick either dark blue, grey or black. Pick a classical cut for the suit. Guys this means two buttons, girls keep it simple. Make sure that the suit fits you well. It does not have to be tailored but try a few different brands and cuts before you settle on one. It should not hang off you but instead should be in keeping with your natural frame.

Guys, wear a shirt and tie that are unfussy and clean. I would suggest a white shirt and a simple dark tie with nothing eccentric on it. You do not want to appear quirky. You want to look like a serious lawyer. Girls, a tailored white shirt is great, but watch that cleavage. You want your interviewer to be paying attention to what you're saying not admiring your other features.

Cufflinks should be simple and not a talking point. No pocket squares, this is not Ascot. Shoes should be black without exception and of a simple design. Girls no massive heels. If you feel conscious of your height and feel like you really need them for your confidence then fine, but no stilettos.

Underlying all of the above is a need for good execution. You have been dressing yourselves for years you say (and I would agree with you) yet you would be amazed at how many people turn up to interview wearing a tie but with the top button undone and a bit loosened, or their shoes un-polished. This gives the strong impression that they are recovering from a night out and does not impress. Make sure there is no gap between your tie and your collar and make sure your shoes shine like bowling balls.

Absolutely no aftershave or perfume. This is not a date. You are not trying to seduce your interviewer with your scent.

Final comment on dress is a subtle one. I have said spend as much as possible but that comes with a caveat. You want to look well-dressed, smart and professional. Do not try to look too flash. You are being interviewed by someone who works very hard for their living and enjoys a good standard of life, but they had to work to get there and have to work even harder to stay there. If you look richer than your interviewer you risk making him/her think you are a rich kid who already has it all and is undeserving of a shot to make it big as a lawyer.

Think, if you were the interviewer, who would you rather give a shot to? A flash rich kid or someone who is really trying to come up in the world? Who is likely to work harder? So dress well, but don't go over the top. If you buy designer, it should not be obviously designer (no obvious labels or designer prints). Again save that until you have the job offer, then go nuts.

Quick recap

Okay I think you have the idea. Dress to impress. Look like you already work there. Don't try and outshine the person interviewing you with designer bling, but instead look clean, smart and co-ordinated. Dressing well will even make you feel more like you already work there, and less like you are an imposter. Do not underestimate how important your appearance is. Look great.

Chapter 13

The big day

"There were those who said this day would never come. What have they to say now?"

Anon.

It is here, finally. All those months of preparation are over and it is finally your time to shine. You will feel nervous, that is normal. If you don't feel nervous you don't care enough and you need to watch that. It is better to be feeling nervous because you will take the most care with your behaviour and your responses. With that in mind, there are some things you can do to control your anxiety and make sure that you enter the office putting your best foot forward, which I set out below.

Conduct a recce – before the big day, find out where the office is. Then find a café nearby that serves food. You need to know exactly how long it would take you to get from the café to the office. Ideally you only want to be five minutes walking distance away.

Get accommodation - if you don't live in London, make sure that you are there the night before. Stay in a hotel. It may cost you £100 but it is worth the peace of mind. Trains have been known to be delayed and you could miss your interview because of this. It may not be your fault, but the guy who came up the night before made his interview.

Eat something - On the day, if the interview is in the morning go and get breakfast at a nearby café. Read the FT, touching up your knowledge on the key issues of the day. It goes without saying that you should handle your breakfast like rods of plutonium. You don't want the lid of your medium caffè latte to peel off and cover you in burning shame. It happens, but not to you. If you don't feel like food on the day, take a banana or cereal bar. You need to eat something or you will feel faint.

Listen to music - if you know a motivational song from playing sport that will get you gee'd up (think "Eye of the Tiger" or almost anything from the Rocky soundtrack or whatever works for you), when you are having your breakfast put it on. Get "in the zone" or get your "game face" on or something equally appropriate.

After you have had your light breakfast go to the toilets to check yourself in the mirror. Nothing stuck in your teeth? Back of your suit jacket collar down? Did you remember the breath mints? Of course you did. Pop 'em now.

You already know exactly how long it will take you to get from the café to your interview. Now it's time to go. You want to arrive at the office 10 minutes early. Any more and you look like you can't keep time, any less and you risk being thrown straight into the interview before you have had time to adjust to your surroundings.

When you arrive at the office, go and introduce yourself to reception. Check that you are at the right entrance if there is more than one. The receptionists will know you are coming and will be able to point out where you need to go. As you are ten minutes early you will likely be told to take a seat and wait till you are called. Be cool. Smile.

If you are offered a drink at this point, politely decline. The café should have topped up your liquid levels and a drink at this point will be another potential thing to fluster you if someone comes to get you mid-way through your cappuccino, and is a final opportunity to spill something down your front.

I would advise against reading the paper, because again, it will be something that you have to consciously fold and put down when someone comes to get you. So just sit tight, try not to fidget or nail bite and wait. Best scenario is that there are other interviewees there in a similar position that look more nervous than you. Talk to them and take solace in the fact that you are already not the most nervous one there.

When someone comes to get you, it will probably be a current trainee sent to put you at ease. This person will have no say in whether you are employed or not (unless you say something which gives them reason to report you) so you can relax a bit. Be polite, but don't worry about turning on the charm or trying to impress yet. That is about to come.

A final word before I go into how to conduct yourself in the interview, to reassure you. You have made it this far, which means that they already think that you have the potential to work there. You have already passed a thorough and extremely rigorous screening process. They will be paying for your travel expenses, so they are already willing to pay you to come to their offices. They want you. All you have to do is show them how keen you are and what a nice person you are to work with to make their decision a no-brainer.

So go and be keen and friendly, don't worry about being word-perfect or coming up with a groundbreaking answer that the interviewer will think is incredibly inspired. All they really want to know is would they want to work with you, and would they be happy putting you in front of a client. Your excellent dress sense will help with the latter, all you have to do now is get on with them. Be humble and be keen to learn but above all, demonstrate a desire to get stuck in.

Behaviour in the interview

This is it, you finally get to meet the person(s) who will decide your fate. Your first interview will more than likely be with someone from HR who is there to ease you into the process and to ask all the questions about you, your background, teamwork and leadership experience and so on. The easier questions if you like. You could however skip this step and be thrown straight into the partner or panel interview. Regardless, your first impression is vital.

I strongly suggest that you practise what I am going to lay out below. Do it with a friend or family member, or someone on your course who is also interviewing. Practice makes perfect and it will help you discover your weak points that you need to work on.

When you meet your interviewer, shake hands and smile and repeat their name back to them when you say hello. This is a polite touch, shows confidence and above all will subconsciously help you remember it for when you say goodbye.

How you shake hands is vital for the first impression. What you are aiming for is a confident firm grip and two shakes. Do not put your hand out horizontally to try and be on top of theirs (this is a business trick to make you seem in control as they are forced to place their hand underneath yours). Do not use both hands. Do not put your hand on their shoulder as you shake. You are not a politician.

The biggest problem is people not gripping firmly enough. This makes you look like a wet egg and either so completely insecure that you cannot squeeze another human's hand, or so above the person that you cannot be bothered to expend the energy making their acquaintance. The best example of this I have encountered was a student grasping my offered hand with two fingers and a thumb with a sort of lazy flicking gesture, as one might throw down a soiled rag. This does not make a good impression.

When you shake their hand look them in the eye and smile. The origin of the handshake was to show that you were not armed and that you were a trustworthy individual. While the former reason (in the UK at least) has less relevance, the latter is still very strong. If you look someone in the eyes and smile it shows confidence, that you have nothing to hide and that you are keen to engage with them. It is attractive. But remember this is not a date so no winking or lip biting.

Next, be professional. The interviewer, if he or she is good, will try immediately to put you at ease asking how your journey was and raising any topical banter. Give an outward impression of being relaxed, but on the inside you should be tracking your every word. By all means have a joke, in fact I would encourage this, but know where to draw the line. Where is the line I hear you ask? I believe it was a Supreme Court judge who said that you will know it when you see it. I hope the same will apply to you.

Learning what professional behaviour is and how to act in a big law firm can only be learnt with experience. For now err on the side of caution and be polite but restrained.

Quick recap

Pay attention to your handshake and practise it beforehand. Practise introducing yourself to people and make sure you always look them in the eye and smile confidently. Say your name clearly and repeat theirs back to them to help you remember it. Now that you have that clear in your mind it is one less thing to think about. Next we get down to some examples of the actual questions and some suggested answers.

Chapter 14

Potential interview questions and ideas for answers

This section is designed to give you a glimpse of what is coming. These questions will almost certainly appear in some form and you should be prepared for them. Make sure you have practised a response to each of these topic headings and have an idea of what you will say. These responses will need to be tweaked on the day so that you respond to the interviewer's specific questions. The example responses are for information purposes only and should not be used as responses in an actual interview.

Why are you interested in working for us?

You should say what aspects about that firm appeal to you. Which of their core values do you feel tie in with your own? What is it that you like about their strategy and why do you want to be a part of it? Draw on what you have picked up from their website. Name-drop people you have met already from the firm either at an open day or at a law fair.

For example: "I really enjoyed talking to x at the York law fair about a recent transaction that he has been working on involving y. Since talking to him I have read up on more of the detail of the deal and was particularly interested by how the parties managed to push the deal through despite so much opposition from z. I would be really keen to find out more about what happened on the inside that made that possible." This is much more convincing than someone who has only read the website and also it reminds them who you are and that they met you at the law fair.

You need to get across that you really have a desire to work for them and not just any law firm. Appeal to their egos and describe back to them what they claim sets them apart. Make sure you do your homework and really understand the values they are promoting.

Why commercial law?

This is obviously one of the big ones and is a good one to have really practised beforehand. What you need to get across to your interviewer is that you understand: a) what commercial law involves; b) what the lawyer's job involves; and c) who the clients are and what they expect. Essentially you need to talk about the lawyer's role in commercial transactions, illustrated with examples and how you find it interesting.

In answering the question I suggest that you talk about a particular deal or subject that you have read about in the press that you have found interesting. This way you can use aspects of that deal to illustrate the different aspects of commercial law that appeal to you.

For example you could describe a deal involving a merger of two competing companies that was able to be completed despite a strong potential for it to lead to market dominance.

The lawyer's role was to assist the parties in c
competition authorities that there would not be ،
monopoly being created, perhaps by carving out
business being acquired (e.g. selling subsidiaries
countries where it would lead to a monopoly) to   ., the
deal to go through.

You could say how you found that very interesting, and that
you like that there was such a need for creative investigation
of the client's business, a need for a close working relationship
and how the law firm delivered an innovative solution that
benefited all parties.

Make sure above all that you communicate that you
understand the relationship between the law firms and their
clients and how it is the client's needs that drive the whole
process.

**Please could you describe to me a deal that you have been
following recently in the market? What impact has this had
on the market generally?**

If you have been carrying out the research like I have
suggested, you should genuinely have some deals that you
have found interesting for one reason or another. The
interviewer will almost definitely have your application form
answers in front of him, so be prepared to expand on the deal
you talked about there.

Tip: If possible talk about a deal or issue that is not
mainstream (this applies to your application form as well).
This will show that you have delved enough into the financial
press to find some of the less talked-about areas and haven't
just read the headlines (although an awareness of the big
issues is still very important).

there is the added bonus that your interviewer may not have heard of the issue so you may be able to explain it to him. This is great, because if your memory on some of the smaller details is sketchy you are less likely to be caught out with the dreaded "are you sure that's correct?"

If you are asked about a specific deal that has gone completely under your radar then don't panic. Rather than waffle vagaries, deflect the question and say something like "ah yes, I've read about that, but to be honest not in too much detail. I have however followed x really closely that was set in a very similar context" and then go on to talk about that. Obviously this is not ideal, but is better than trying to wing it when you have no idea.

Unlike an exam, the questions in an interview (as previously mentioned) are designed to give you a springboard to show your interviewer what you are capable of in terms of market understanding. It is not too important if you missed one deal (especially if it is not very mainstream) what is more important is that you can talk about an issue that you do know about with interest, passion and understanding.

In terms of the lawyer's role in commercial transactions, you can say how you like the idea of advising a client at the formative stages of a transaction's development, for example on how to structure an acquisition. Should it be by way of a new special purpose vehicle subsidiary, or a joint venture with an existing subsidiary? Then as the transaction progresses, how you would enjoy guiding a client through a process which is often very unfamiliar to them in a high-pressure environment. How, if something unexpected cropped up at the last minute, you would enjoy having to think on your feet to adapt and create a solution that may never have been done before.

As to the deal's impact on the market, it may be nothing or a lot. If it is a ground-breaking transaction, such as the Kraft Cadbury takeover, it may set a precedent for future similar transactions. If it is a small niche deal, it may not seem to have affected the market at all, but you could say that it has set a precedent for a deal of that nature, which would be relevant if similar facts occurred on a larger scale, which could have an effect on the market.

When did you first consider a career in law? What steps have you taken to explore this as a possibility?

Obviously the earlier that you considered a career in law the better in terms of showing long-term commitment. For most though, depending on your degree, it is either in the last few years of school (when you are choosing your A-levels with a degree in law in mind) or in the first two years of university. For those who take the path of the GDL then it is fine to say at university.

As to what steps you have taken, this is a chance for you to show off your work experience. Also discuss your law fair visits and open days as well as any people you have spoken to find out more about a career in commercial law.

Tell me a situation where you have received negative feedback. How did you handle that?

Everyone who starts as a trainee solicitor will receive negative feedback because at the beginning you get things wrong when you don't really know what you are doing. You need to be able to show you can handle being told you are not hitting the mark and learn from it and most of all not take it personally or react badly.

An example would be "I gave a presentation at university and was told by my tutor afterwards that I spoke far too fast and was difficult to follow. I admit I didn't like being told this as I had always thought I was good at presentations, but after asking some of the other students they agreed my tutor was right.

Rather than getting upset, I decided to practise future presentations paying particular attention to how fast I spoke and on timing. I found that this extra practice made me more comfortable with the material, and therefore more comfortable as a presenter. Once I felt in command of the subject I was much more relaxed and able to speak slowly and clearly. I learnt that at the end of the day my tutor was right, and if she had not told me I would have continued giving bad presentations for the rest of my degree."

Equally, examples drawing on criticism of your written work would be very appropriate because this is a classic for new trainees. Most think they can write well, but few know how to write in the correct style for work. Some do not react well when they are told that their writing style is wrong and needs to change. Show that you are prepared for this.

What do you see is the future for this firm? Where do you think we should expand? How should we do that?

The firm's website will give you details of what the current strategy of the firm is. The law fair is also a great opportunity to ask how each firm distinguishes itself from the competition and what the future goals are.

Check where there are current offices. This is often overlooked but regularly comes up when you are asked where the firm should contemplate expanding.
Think generally about what/where the new emerging markets are. Think that if there is a very obvious country (e.g. India)

where there are no offices but seem like there should be, why there are not? Are there any barriers to entry? In the case of India, in case you did not know, foreign law firms have been banned from opening offices since a 1995 High Court ruling. So don't say India!

Consider that there are two principal ways of expanding. These are either organically or through lateral hires. On a small scale, organic growth is by means of hiring more people at graduate level and training them so that they progress their careers at the firm and in turn cause it to grow. Lateral hiring means hiring an already qualified lawyer or team of lawyers usually from another similar firm to bolster an expanding practice group. On a global level this is interpreted as either opening a new office of the firm and sending people there from other established offices (organic) or by merging with a current "best-friend" firm (one with which the firm already has significant relations and experience).

Who else are you interviewing with?

They expect that you will be interviewing with other firms. Keep the list short and relevant. Similar firms will show that you are sure about the type of place you want to work/the type of work.

Give me an example of leadership, teamwork, working under pressure or to a tight deadline or problem solving.

These are based on individual experience and are really worth thinking about before you go to interview. Make sure you have examples from work experience as well as from university. Any other fundraising or charity work that you have done where you had deadlines and targets and were required to lead or work as part of a team will clearly be relevant. Have a think about how you are going to present each story you have, what the good points of it are that demonstrate leadership, initiative, team-playing, resourcefulness, dedication and morale building.

Think that the interviewer is trying to imagine how you would cope working in different circumstances playing different roles. On one transaction you might be required to lead a team of other trainees who have just been drafted in last minute under pressure, while also taking direction from your supervisor. You need to be both a team player and a leader. So think of situations that evidence both.

Chapter 15

Interview tips

To assist you further with the interview here is a collection of practical ideas I have picked up from discussions with my colleagues and graduate recruitment teams.

Be yourself

This is a classic adage oft repeated, but it is true. Although it is clear that you want to present yourself in the most professional way, don't try to be someone you are not. The interview process is two way and it is for you to decide if you would fit in well at that firm as much as it is for them to decide whether to make you an offer. If the firm is very straight-laced and academic and you as an individual tend to be a bit more outgoing, don't feel that you need to act exactly like them at interview.

If you try to act like someone you are not and you are hired on the basis of that, you will risk not enjoying the job itself as you will not be with like-minded people. Also you will have enough to be thinking about without adding personality adjustment to the list.

Water please

When you arrive in the interview room, always ask for a glass of water. Firstly you are going to be doing a lot of talking so will need to stay moist, you don't want to end up with cotton-mouth. Secondly, having a glass of water is a great opportunity to give yourself some thinking space. When the interviewer asks you a question you are not sure how to answer, pick up the glass and take a sip while you think. If need be take two.

These extra 5 – 10 seconds can make a big difference and it makes you look like a calm person in control. If you run out of water ask for more. Whatever you do, don't pick up an empty glass and take a sip. It sounds obvious, but I have been told people really do this and it looks awful.

Pause before engaging

When you are asked a question always pause and formulate an answer before you start speaking. In conversation silences can be awkward and are to be avoided, but it is much better in an interview to pause thoughtfully than to dive in using lots of umms and errrs. Never, ever say either of these. If you are a natural ummer and errer you need to practise not doing it.

Be in control of what you say and dispense with gap fillers, they will only serve to make you look like you don't know what to say. Someone told me that as preparation they tried playing that BBC radio game "Just a Minute", where you have to talk about a topic without pausing, repeating yourself or saying umm or err. It is very difficult and as such, good training.

Take time to think when you don't know

If you don't know the answer straight away, say "do you mind if I take a minute to think about that?" They will always say that it's fine. There is no need to answer immediately. Then actually think about the answer. If you still don't know after 30 seconds or so, or think of anything that might reasonably be crafted into relevance, you can do one of two things:

1. An outright admission that you don't know. This is fine if the question is on a specific area like a recent deal that you have not studied, but less okay if it is more general like what is your favourite book. Try not to say that you don't know too often though.

2. In addition to saying you don't know, what will make you stand out as a candidate is if you turn the question onto a subject that you do know something about, as I have mentioned earlier. For instance, say "to be honest I haven't studied that particular deal very closely, but it might be similar to this deal about [...]" and then give your opinion / answer in relation to the deal that you do know about.

As previously mentioned, interviewers have a set of questions designed to get you talking and to allow you to demonstrate that you have what it takes. They are, with some very limited exceptions, not out to trip you up and instead are trying to give you an opportunity to shine. They have sat in your position before and know that it is not a fun place to be. So if you don't know exactly what they are referring to, slickly switch onto something you do know about and show them how great you are.

Do not lie or make things up

The interviewer will already have an answer in mind if he is asking you a question of fact. Inventing things or waffling around a subject will only show your interviewer that you are capable of imaginative invention, which in some instances is important, but mostly in law you are not meant to make up the answers.

How long do you talk for?

A good interviewer, once they have asked the question will let you run with it, often without telling you when to stop. So how long should you talk for? Again no hard and fast rule, but probably no more than one or two minutes. Learning to stop is a key skill. If you are not sure if you have answered the question don't be afraid to say "Has that answered your question?" If they say no, then ask on which bit they feel they could use more elaboration.

This is a great technique, and far better than just stopping and leaving it hanging there when you could have completely missed the point. Asking will give you a second chance to get it right. Of course they may just say that you have answered it. In which case, take a sip of water and get ready for the next question.

Answering questions

When asked about who you are and your past, you will want to impress your interviewer, that much is obvious. But there is a way to do it. You will be bursting to list all of your achievements, but I urge you to hold back. If, as a general point, you can come across as humble but brilliant, it will stand you in good stead. Humble people tend to lead with something that they did not do so well. This has a natural humanising effect. When you have demonstrated that you have not always initially nailed it, you can casually mention that you have absolutely learnt by past experience and now you are on top of it. So save your best until last. That way you will come across as humble, but strong.

Ask your interviewer questions

After you have answered a question, you can always say "What do you think about that?" or "Do you agree?" or even "Have you ever had a similar experience?" This is great because it again shows confidence and is a way to break down the question/answer structure and make it more of a dialogue. Don't ask anything that you should already know from basic research, for example if the firm has any offices in France, if it is clear that they do indeed have an office in Paris. Don't ask random questions for the sake of it, but rather try and make them an extension of your earlier dialogue.

Be able to improvise

Preparation is vital, but don't try to learn answers to questions. You should know what you will say when asked "Why a career in law?" but not the exact formulation of how you are going to say it. If you try and learn a speech it will sound stilted and chances are you will be nervous and make a mess of it. What you ideally want are lots of phrases and things to say all jumbled up in your head that you can pluck out as and when necessary.

Practise alone in your room, talking as if you are answering an interview question. It will feel weird at first and you will be very conscious of your own voice but once you relax into it will show you the areas you are comfortable talking about and the areas where you are struggling to find something to say. When you identify areas you are not so good on, make a note and come back to them. The aim here is not to keep going over what you are good at, but to force yourself to practise those areas on which you feel weakest.

At the end, it's your turn to ask the questions

When the interview is drawing to a close, the interviewer will usually invite you to ask any of your questions. This is not something to be passed up, you should have some questions ready. If you managed to find out who was interviewing you before the interview and managed to research the deals he has worked on this is your moment to shine.

Nowadays it is rare that you will know who you will be facing, so keeping your questions general to the firm is fine. Ideally you will have touched on something already in the dialogue that you can expand on with a question at the end, such as "What was your experience / take on that when it happened?"

It's over...

When it is over, go home and give yourself another pat on the back. If you nailed it, chances are that you will hear from them very soon. If you didn't it will be a few days. Law firms are traditionally much better than investment banks at actually calling people up after and telling them that they did not make the cut.

If you do get the "thanks but no thanks" call, make sure you ask the graduate recruitment team for specifics of where you went wrong. Remember, even if you don't make it, the interview will have been great practice and you can learn a lot about what you have to improve, provided you check. Don't waste the chance to learn because you are too shy to ask.

Chapter 16

Skype interview tips

Video calling interviews, most commonly referred to as Skype interviews, are far from an ideal method to meet your future employers. They feel artificial, place an additional barrier between you and your interviewer and are an extra obstacle in your path to impress them. Although you will probably have used Skype or some other video calling software before, for personal conversations, an interview using the same technology has a very different feel to it. There is always the fear that the connection will degrade and the slightest blip in the call can serve to set you off balance.

In addition to the Skype interview there is also a new form of pre-interview screening called Launchpad. The idea is that a law firm can set a number of questions and, by getting the candidate to use a webcam, record their timed responses. There is an option to allow the candidate to re-record the response or to restrict each response to one attempt. Law firms have very mixed feelings about whether this is a useful tool and most recognise it as a very artificial way of selecting a potential colleague. At the time of writing only one firm is using it.

In this section I set out some guidance that has been gleaned from conversations with recent interviewees and graduate recruitment staff. Most issues affect both parties. It is in everybody's interest that the technology works and that the focus can be on the candidate's suitability, not on understanding what he or she is trying to say.

Tips

Prepare as you would for a standard interview - you should expect the nature of the questions to be just the same as if you were there in person. A video interview is by no means an easier option.

Look the part - dress as you would for an in-person interview (both top and bottom). Before the interview, practise sitting in your outfit in front of the camera to make sure that you look okay. Ladies watch out for backlighting making blouses see-through and men no reflective tie patterns or suit fabrics.

Prepare your surroundings - that means no clutter around you and a clean light-coloured background with no distracting images. Ensure there is a decent amount of light directed onto your face (not too much top-down light, as it will put your eyes in shadow). Remove all personal items from view including photos, mascots and so on.

Check your I.T. is working - your internet connection needs to be fast enough to support a good -quality visual feed (not necessarily in high definition). Be sure to restart your computer so that it is fresh and responsive and if you are using a laptop make sure it is plugged in. Ensure you have downloaded the latest version of your video calling software.

Finally, sign in to your Skype account long before the call in case you have any log-in issues with your account.

Isolate yourself - inform anyone you share a living space with about the interview with strict instructions that you are not to be disturbed.

Practise the interview first - get used to speaking in front of a webcam. Record your attempts with software such as Call Recorder that integrates with Skype.

Smile – this is harder than when you are face-to-face, so make sure that you don't neglect to do it and that you are not just staring wide-eyed at the camera.

Look at the camera not the picture of yourself – this gives the impression of eye-contact and makes a big difference to how you connect with your interviewers.

Reassure your interviewers that you are listening - use more audio cues than you would face-to-face to show that you are engaged in order to reassure your counterparts that the connection is still established and that you are not playing Pacman®.

Never type anything on your keyboard or fiddle during a call – if you need to take notes write them down, the sound of tapping is very distracting.

No crib sheets - you have the opportunity to "cheat" on a video call by having some notes in front of you off-camera to help you if you get stuck. Whilst this advice is given by some people, I would strongly argue against it, as you will look odd glancing down and may feel obligated to look if a question comes up on something that you have notes on. You won't be expected to remember lots of statistical information and everything else you should have memorised before the call.

Houston, it's broken - in the event of any technology failing, address the issue immediately. It is better to say "Sorry to interrupt but my connection is failing. Can I hang-up and call you back?" than to struggle on hoping it will get better. In the event of a complete technology fail, email your HR contact immediately to explain and reschedule another interview.

Chapter 17

Summary and conclusion

"We are what we repeatedly do. Excellence, therefore, is not an act but a habit"

Aristotle

So how do you feel? Overwhelmed? Or raring to go? I hope it is the latter! In this book I have set out the key points that you need to think about in order to get a training contract. Just to recap these are:

Qualify - get the right qualifications, whether this is an undergraduate law degree followed by the LPC, or a non-law undergraduate degree followed by the GDL and then the LPC.

Type of law - think about what area of law you want to go into, the type of firm you want to work for and the type of work you want to do. Use the sources I have suggested and consult with people who are in the know to find out more about your options.

Choose your firms - once you have an idea of what you want to do, find out which firms specialise in the type of law you want to go into and start researching them at a high level.

Organisation - draw up a plan to help you keep track of relevant dates relating to vacation schemes, open days, law fairs and training contract applications.

General research - start your background market research, use a folder or stick articles to the wall. Either way start to read a lot about what is going on with the big corporates and banks. Research and understand the jargon and make sure you are comfortable explaining industry specific terms at interview.

Experience - start getting work experience as soon as possible, whether this is through a vacation scheme or an ad-hoc placement with a high street firm.

Law fairs - go to your university's law fair and meet the people you might one day be working with. Ask relevant questions that you cannot find the answer to through consulting their published material. Make an impression and be memorable (for the right reasons...)

Targeted research - thoroughly research your chosen law firms and the environment they operate in.

Apply - complete your training contract application form and have it thoroughly checked for errors or omissions. Once submitted make sure you get a confirmatory e-mail recording its receipt. Don't be afraid to pick up the phone and call graduate recruitment if you are unsure.

Interview - go to the interview and put into practice the tips I have outlined in this book. Remember preparation is key!

Follow up - if it all goes wrong at either the application or interview stage, make sure you follow up with graduate recruitment, this is not a time to feel shy. Make sure that a failed attempt becomes a vital learning experience that you use to enable you to succeed at your next try.

Well, that's it for now. I hope this book has been of some help. In addition to the practical guidance that I have set out, I hope what this book will give you is the confidence that you can succeed, and more importantly, the will to try. Do not be put off if you do not succeed the first time, rejection is statistically more likely than acceptance, so expect to be rejected more than you succeed. Don't take it personally, or allow it to make you question whether or not you are cut out for this. You are, maybe you just need to work on how you show it a bit more. But that's okay, you just started right?

If it goes wrong repeatedly with one firm, don't be disheartened. It may be that you genuinely don't have what they are looking for. Again, try not to take this personally, all firms have their strict criteria and just because you don't have exactly what they are looking for does not mean that you are any less suited to a career as a solicitor as a result. I know many current colleagues were rejected by one or more of the firms they applied to and yet they have gone on to become very successful solicitors.

If you are rejected by everyone you apply to, call the graduate recruitment teams and try and find out what it is that you are doing wrong (you may be being very consistent!) If it is a question of your academic results holding you back, try and see if you can retake exams to bolster your marks. If you lack work experience go out and get more. If you need more extra-curricular activities to bolster your CV do something extra-curricular. Almost all the weak points for which candidates are rejected can be addressed and rectified, the key is to find out what it is that you need to fix. Once you know, get busy.

Above all don't give up. You may be one application form away from a successful hire and a life-changing job. Wouldn't you kick yourself if you never filled it out because of previous failure? Stay at it. Be determined that you would be great for that job and let them know it.

Now get out there and start putting into practice what I have set out here. Go and buy the FT and the Economist. Work out time in your schedule that you can set aside for the purpose of your research, and the timings of when the application deadlines are. They are your goals so everything else needs to fit around those dates. Start today!

I wish you every success!

Best

James

Let me know if you want any further one-to-one tuition, I am now offering an interview coaching service and application form review.

We can discuss your strengths and weaknesses and make sure that you put your best foot forward! Send me an email at **james.howard1910@gmail.com** to find out more.